EDGE BOOKS

D0477068

MINI-BEAST WARS

PRAYING MANTIS VS GIANT HORNET

BY ALICIA Z. KLEPEIS

BATTLE OF THE POWERFUL PREDATORS

Raintree is an imprint of Capstone Global Library Limited, a company incorporated in England and Wales having its registered office at 264 Banbury Road, Oxford, OX2 7DY – Registered company number: 6695582

www.raintree.co.uk
myorders@raintree.co.uk

Printed and bound in China.

ISBN 978 1 4747 1087 9 (hardback)
20 19 18 17 16
10 9 8 7 6 5 4 3 2 1

ISBN 978 1 4747 1091 6 (paperback)
20 19 18 17 16 15
10 9 8 7 6 5 4 3 2 1

British Library Cataloguing in Publication Data
A full catalogue record for this book is available from the British

Editorial Credits
Nate LeBoutillier, editor; Russell Griesmer, designer; Katy LaVigne, production specialist

The publisher would like to thank Christiane Welrauch, Professor of Entomology at University of California, Riverside for her help creating this book.

Photo Credits
Getty Images: Digital Vision, 13 (left), 25, 27; James P. Rowan, 29; Minden Pictures: FLPA/S & D & K Maslowski, Cover (left), Cover (back), 5, Nature Production/Satoshi Kuribayashi, Cover (right), 4, 6, 9 (top), 11 (top), 21 (top); Newscom: Minden Pictures/Michael Durham, 11 (bottom); Science Source: Lawrence Lawry, 17, Scott Camazine, 24; Shutterstock: Cristian Gusa, 13 (right), Cristian Gusa, 19 (bottom), Cristian Gusa, 22, Evgeniy Ayupov, 9 (bottom), 23, pattara puttiwong, 7, POPUMON, 15, Stubblefield Photography, 19 (top); UIG via Getty Images/Education Images, 21 (bottom)

Design Elements
Capstone and Shutterstock:

VS CONTENTS

WELCOME TO MINI-BEAST WARS! 4

THE COMBATANTS 6

SIZE 8

SPEED AND AGILITY 10

DEFENCES 12

PRAYING MANTIS WEAPONS 14

GIANT HORNET WEAPONS 16

WEAKNESSES 18

ATTACK STYLE 20

GET READY TO RUMBLE! 22

THE BATTLE BEGINS! 24

GLOSSARY 30

READ MORE 31

WEBSITES 31

INDEX 32

WELCOME TO MINI-BEAST WARS!

A mini-beast can be a savage creature. It searches for **prey**, finds it and goes in for the kill. Sometimes one mini-beast can easily overpower its victim. A crafty spider might catch an unsuspecting fly in its web. A single Asian giant hornet has been known to kill 40 honey bees per minute. That's one corpse every 1.5 seconds! But in Mini-Beast Wars, there's no clear winner. Carnivores attack other **carnivores**. Giant mini-beasts take on other huge insects. All kinds of mini-beast battles are possible!

In this mini-beast war, the praying mantis and the Asian giant hornet battle it out – to the death. You will find out how these immense insects match up. You'll discover what weapons they possess and how they use them to fight. Then you'll watch them battle antennae to antennae!

FIERCE FACT

AFRICA'S KALAHARI BUSHMEN BELIEVE THE MANTIS IS SACRED AND THAT IT REPRESENTS THE GOD OF CREATION.

prey animal hunted by another animal for food

carnivore animal that eats meat

THE COMBATANTS

The Chinese mantis is one species of about 2,400 different species of praying mantises around the world. It may not actually fight very often with the Asian giant hornet. But both terrifying insects live in China, Japan and other parts of Asia. They are some of the largest mini-beasts in the whole of Asia. Each of these fierce insects can cause an enemy serious pain.

The Chinese mantis crunches all kinds of creatures. It makes meals of insects, lizards and even hummingbirds.

Asian giant hornets often destroy their fellow insects quite easily. They sometimes hunt in groups. Just 30 Asian giant hornets can completely wipe out a colony housing 10,000 European honey bees in an hour. Talk about a massacre!

These two predators might not choose to hunt each other much. After all, they could easily prey on smaller insects. But you never know – these hungry mini-beasts look for food anywhere they can find it!

CHINESE MANTIDS ARRIVED IN THE
UNITED STATES IN THE LATE 1800S.
THEY WERE, PERHAPS, STOWAWAYS ON
A BOAT THAT WAS SHIPPING PLANTS.
TODAY THE CHINESE MANTIS IS THE
LARGEST AND MOST COMMONLY SEEN
MANTIS IN THE UNITED STATES.

species   group of animals with similar features

predator   animal that hunts other animals for food

SIZE

The Chinese mantis is a large, strong predator. It measures up to 12.7 centimetres (5 inches) long. That's about as long as a mobile phone. Its wingspan averages about 8 to 10 cm (3 to 4 in) long. Despite its large size, the Chinese mantis is a lightweight. At roughly 3 grams (0.11 ounces), it's as heavy as a penny. The Chinese mantis' size and strength could overpower most insect enemies.

The Asian giant hornet is the world's largest hornet species. Worker and drone Asian hornets measure about 3.6 cm (1.4 in) long. That's roughly the size of a child's thumb. The queen's body is bigger at more than 5 cm (2 in) long. This hornet's wingspan could spread over the width of your hand at roughly 8 cm (3 in) wide. The Asian giant hornet weighs 20 times as much as a honey bee. Although it's smaller than the Chinese mantis, the giant hornet's size makes it difficult to defeat in a fight.

RATING

3.5

ASIAN GIANT HORNET:
big buzzer

RATING

4

CHINESE MANTIS:
long lunger

FIERCE FACT

IN JAPAN, ASIAN GIANT HORNETS ARE REFERRED TO AS "SPARROW WASPS" BECAUSE THEY ARE SO LARGE THAT THEY RESEMBLE SMALL BIRDS.

SPEED AND AGILITY

The Chinese mantis takes its time – until it's ready to strike. Its average walking speed is slower than a three-toed sloth's. Mantids usually only fly to escape a predator or to get to a new perch. Their slow cruising speed while in flight is only about half as fast as the bats which hunt them.

But when snaring prey, the Chinese mantis moves super speedily. A mantis strike has been measured at 30 to 50 one-thousandths of a second. How fast is this? A mantis could strike twice in the time it takes you to blink your eye!

Asian giant hornets aren't fast on their feet. They usually only walk when they're building their ground-level nests.

The Asian giant hornet is a much faster flyer than its mantis enemy. It can cruise the skies at 40 kilometres (25 miles) per hour. That's speedier than most adults can cycle down a steep hill. This flight speed is a real advantage when tracking down prey. They can cover 80 to 95 km (50 to 60 miles) a day while flying.

RATING |||||| **5**

ASIAN GIANT HORNET:
furious flier

RATING |||||| **3**

CHINESE MANTIS:
speedy striker

FIERCE FACT

ASIAN GIANT HORNETS WILL CHASE HUMANS. THEY
ARE VERY ATTRACTED TO HUMAN SWEAT, FAST
MOVEMENTS AND SWEET SMELLS.

DEFENCES

The Chinese mantis has a tough **exoskeleton**. This protects its insides if attacked. The mantis' bulging **compound eyes** give it excellent vision. They allow it to see in several directions at once. They also help judge distances very accurately – up to 20 metres (65 feet) away, an amazing distance for an insect.

The Chinese mantis has great **camouflage** to keep it hidden from predators and prey. Its pale green or tan hue blends in with the plants it lives on. Its long, skinny body resembles a twig that sways. Even its wings look like thin leaves.

Just like its enemy, the Asian giant hornet has antennae that gather sensory information. The hornet can also see in multiple directions at once.

Unlike the Chinese mantis, the Asian giant hornet doesn't blend into the background. Instead, its bright yellow-orange colouring serves a protective purpose. It tells potential predators, "Stay away – I'm **toxic**!"

The Asian giant hornet can stay out of sight. Its nests are often built underground or in tree hollows. But if it buzzes out, other mini-beasts should beware!

IN AUSTRALIA AND AFRICA, WHERE BUSH FIRES OFTEN SWEEP THROUGH THE LANDSCAPE, PRAYING MANTIDS HAVE BEEN KNOWN TO CHANGE COLOUR WITHIN A FEW DAYS. THIS HELPS THEM MATCH THE CHARCOAL HUES OF THE BURNED LANDSCAPE.

RATING 2.5

ASIAN GIANT HORNET:
toxic tinted

RATING 3

CHINESE MANTIS:
cagey camouflager

exoskeleton structure on the outside of an animal that gives it support

compound eyes eyes made up of many tiny lenses densely packed together

camouflage pattern or colour on an animal's skin that helps it blend in with the things around it

toxic poisonous

PRAYING MANTIS WEAPONS

The Chinese mantis has strong, folded **forelegs**. These can spring into action at lightning speed. Mantids can even grab flying insects from out of the air. Its forelegs feature an array of hooks and spines arranged to serve as a trap.

After catching its prey, the Chinese mantis may even nibble strips of flesh away while its prey is still alive. They can **decapitate** an enemy faster than you can say "Look out!"

FIERCE FACT

AT ONLY 3–5 CM (1–2 IN) LONG, THE SPINY FLOWER MANTIS IS ONE OF THE SMALLER MANTIDS. DESPITE ITS SMALL SIZE, THIS BRIGHTLY-COLOURED MINI-BEAST IS A LIGHTNING-FAST PREDATOR WITH FIRST-RATE HUNTING SKILLS.

RATING
3

CHINESE MANTIS:
champion chewer

foreleg front leg

decapitate cut off the head

GIANT HORNET WEAPONS

The Asian giant hornet's stinger packs a serious punch. It's only about the length of an eraser on a pencil. But unlike most bees' stingers, this deadly weapon can be used again and again.

The Asian giant hornet's sting is very painful to prey. Its stinger injects fast-acting **venom**, which is deadly. It destroys red blood cells and can dissolve flesh.

Located on the outside of the hornet's mouth are its **mandibles**. These slice through the bodies of prey. The Asian giant hornet's mandibles cut, chew and tear food apart. They also come in handy when carrying dead victims around.

FIERCE FACT

WHEN PEOPLE ARE STUNG BY ASIAN GIANT HORNETS, THEIR SKIN LOOKS LIKE IT HAS BEEN PIERCED BY BULLET HOLES. ONE VICTIM DESCRIBED HIS GIANT HORNET BITE AS FEELING "LIKE A HOT NAIL THROUGH MY LEG".

RATING

 4

ASIAN GIANT HORNET:
vicious venom

venom   liquid poison made by an animal to kill its prey

mandible   strong mouthpart used for chewing

WEAKNESSES

Even with their wicked weapons, the Chinese mantis and Asian giant hornet aren't totally without weaknesses. Both insects try catching prey off-guard. The sit-and-wait hunting style of the mantis can leave him open to attackers. Waiting for his prey, the mantis might become another predator's meal. Even when retreating, mantids travel slowly. Compared to the hasty hornet, this is tortoise-like! And females, which fly only rarely, are at a major disadvantage. The Chinese mantis also has a weak sense of smell. So it may not sniff what's creeping up behind it.

The Asian giant hornet is fast but has difficulty hiding. Unlike the mantis, the hornet's yellow-orange colour tends to alert enemies. And it only has a stinger at one end of its body. This leaves it vulnerable to an attack from the side or below its abdomen.

FIERCE FACT

AS A LAST RESORT TO ESCAPE A PREDATOR, A MANTIS MAY SACRIFICE ONE OR MORE OF ITS LEGS. A MANTIS WITHOUT FRONT LEGS -- WHICH ARE USED FOR HUNTING -- USUALLY DIES QUICKLY OF STARVATION.

RATING 3

CHINESE MANTIS:
tardy trudger

RATING 3.5

ASIAN GIANT HORNET:
haphazard hider

ATTACK STYLE

The Chinese mantis is a crafty hunter. It blends in with the surrounding vegetation until prey gets close enough. Then the mantis lashes out and quickly grabs its victim. Its spiny front legs pierce the prey and act as a trap. The mantis is likely to start by biting its enemy's head off. But it could also chew through almost any other body part with its strong jaws. The mantid's lightning-quick reflexes and vice-like grip make it a powerful predator.

Sometimes the Asian giant hornet attacks alone. Other times it works in a group. Either way, the end result is often the death of its enemies. The hornet usually captures its prey in flight, using its super-strong mandibles. It practically never stings the prey it's hunting. The hornet usually bites instead. If a bite doesn't do the job, the hornet will sting repeatedly. The hornet's stings flood victims' bodies with deadly venom.

FIERCE FACT

WHEN ATTACKING, ASIAN GIANT HORNET WORKERS MARK THE HONEY BEE HIVES USING CHEMICAL SUBSTANCES CALLED PHEROMONES. THESE CHEMICALS AFFECT THEIR FELLOW HORNETS' BEHAVIOUR, ENCOURAGING THEM TO "GO ON THE WARPATH".

RATING 4

ASIAN GIANT HORNET:
brutal biter

RATING 4

CHINESE MANTIS:
crafty catcher

GET READY TO RUMBLE!

Are you prepared for the big battle? Two mighty mini-beasts are on the prowl. Each hopes to prove it's the toughest, most vicious insect in Asia.

In one corner is the lightning-quick, head-crunching Chinese mantis. He's spiky, large and in charge. In the other corner is his opponent – the Asian giant hornet. Even his name strikes fear into the hearts of humans and other mini-beasts. He's huge, relentless and deadly. Nobody can say for certain which of these extra-enormous mini-beasts will win the fight. But one thing is for sure – the winner will probably be wounded along the way!

ONE LAST THING...

This fight is made up, just like in your favourite films. These two mini-beasts may occasionally fight in nature, but it's hard to say who would win. However, we know these mini-beasts are ferocious fighters. So if you like a good mini-beast battle, this should be a great show!

THE BATTLE BEGINS!

It's a sunny morning out in a flowery field. Birds twitter, crickets chirp and leaves sway in the breeze. Yet this is the setting for what is to be a ferocious battle. Hiding in the tall grass, the Chinese mantis turns its triangular head back and forth. His huge eyes scan the scene. He's hungry. He waits patiently, his spiny forelegs raised and ready.

Suddenly, an Asian giant hornet buzzes by. In a brief stop, the hornet alights on a grassy patch near the mantis. In the blink of an eye, the mantis springs into action. He grabs the hornet with his barbed forelegs. He tries to bite the hornet with his sharp mandibles. But the hornet sends his stinger right through the mantis' exoskeleton. Ouch! The Chinese mantis retreats in pain, reeling from the nasty jab.

FIERCE FACT

IN THE SUMMER OF 2013, ASIAN GIANT HORNETS KILLED 40 PEOPLE AND INJURED MORE THAN 1,600 IN CHINA'S SHAANXI PROVINCE.

AMBUSH!

The mantis recovers. He holds his wings up to appear larger and scarier. His huge wings crackle. They sound like paper rubbing together. But the hornet is furious. His helicopter-like buzzing fills the space between the two enemies. The hornet zooms in to land on a bare patch of soil near the mantis.

Snap!

The mantis springs forward for Round Two, determined to make a kill. His front legs trap the hornet in a vice-like grip.

MANTIDS COME IN MANY SHAPES AND SIZES. SOME LOOK LIKE FLOWERS. SOME LOOK LIKE LEAVES. SOME LOOK LIKE BLADES OF GRASS, STICKS OR SPIKES. MANTIDS' ABILITY TO BLEND IN GIVES THEM A HUGE ADVANTAGE WHEN HIDING OR ATTACKING.

HEADS UP... HEADS OFF!

With his stinger stuck facing away from the mantis, the hornet is at a disadvantage. The hornet tries one more time to sting his rival – but fails. In a matter of milliseconds, the mantis bites off the hornet's head. Chomp! The hornet's legs twitch briefly. Death comes quickly to the giant hornet.

The mantis leaves almost nothing of his giant meal. The hornet's wings flutter to the ground below. The Chinese mantis has devoured his opponent. Licking his chops, he removes any last guts from his front legs, antennae and eyes. The Chinese mantis has taken out one of the fiercest insects in Asia!

GLOSSARY

carnivore animal that eats meat

compound eyes eyes made up of many tiny lenses densely packed together

decapitate cut off the head

exoskeleton structure on the outside of an animal that gives it support

foreleg front leg

mandible strong mouthpart used for chewing

predator animal that hunts other animals for food

prey animal hunted by another animal for food

species group of animals with similar features

toxic poisonous

venom liquid poison made by an animal to kill its prey

READ MORE

Amazing Animal Predators (Animal Superpowers), John Townsend (Raintree, 2013)

Crazy Creepy Crawlies (Extreme Animals), Isabel Thomas (Raintree, 2013)

The Life Cycle of Insects (Life Cycles) Susan Heinrichs Gray (Raintree, 2012)

WEBSITES

www.britannica.com/animal/mantid
Find out more about the many species of mantids, their features and their behaviours.

www.britannica.com/animal/hornet-insect
Find out more about the many species of hornets, their features and their behaviours.

INDEX

Asian Giant Hornet
    antennae 5, 12
    attack style 6, 18, 20, 21
    colouring 12, 18
    flight speed 10, 18
    mandibles 16, 20
    nests 10, 12
    prey 4, 6, 10, 16, 20
    size of 8, 9
    stingers 16, 18, 24, 28
    venom 12, 16, 24
    wingspan 8

carnivores 4

Chinese Mantis
    antennae 5
    attack style 10, 14, 18, 20, 24–29
    camouflage 12, 13, 20, 24, 26
    exoskeleton 12, 24
    eyes 12, 24
    flight 10, 18
    forelegs 14, 18, 20, 24–27
    prey 6, 10, 12, 14, 18, 20
    size 8, 14, 22
    species 6
    walking speed 10, 18
    wingspan 8, 26

habitat 6

"sparrow wasps" 9